Damien of Molokai

Builder of Community

1840–1889
Born in Tremelo, Belgium
Feast Day: May 10
Patronage:
Hawaii and people with leprosy

Text by Barbara Yoffie
Illustrated by Katherine A. Borgatti

Liguori
ONE LIGUORI DRIVE
LIGUORI MO 63057-9999

Dedication

To my family:
my parents Jim and Peg,
my husband Bill,
our son Sam and daughter-in-law Erin,
and our precious grandchildren
Ben, Lucas, and Andrew

To all the children I have had the privilege of
teaching throughout the years.

Imprimi Potest:
Harry Grile, CSsR, Provincial
Denver Province, The Redemptorists

Published by Liguori Publications
Liguori, Missouri 63057

To order, call 800-325-9521
www.liguori.org

p ISBN 978-0-7648-2242-1
e ISBN 978-0-7648-2292-6

Liguori Publications, a nonprofit corporation, is an apostolate of
The Redemptorists. To learn more about The Redemptorists,
visit Redemptorists.com.

Printed in the United States of America
17 16 15 14 13 / 5 4 3 2 1
First Edition

Dear Parents and Teachers:

Saints and Me! is a series of children's books about saints. Six books make up the first set: *Saints of North America.* In this set, each book tells a thought-provoking story about a heavenly hero.

Saints of North America includes the heroic lives of six saints from the United States, Canada, and Mexico. Saints Kateri Tekakwitha and Elizabeth Ann Seton were both born in the United States. Saint Juan Diego was born in Mexico, and Saint André Bessette was from Canada. European missionaries also came to North America to spread the Catholic faith, making it their home while they worked with people in the New World. Saints Rose Philippine Duchesne and Damien de Veuster were missionary saints.

Through the centuries, saints have always been dear to Catholics, but *why*? In most instances, ordinary people were and are transformed by the life of Jesus and therefore model Christ's life for us. It is our Lord who makes ordinary people extraordinary. As your children come to know the saints, it is our hope that they will come to understand and identify that they, too, are *called to be saints.*

Which saint wanted to work with Native Americans? Who wanted to work with the sick people on the island of Molokai, Hawaii? To which saint did the Virgin Mary appear? Who loved Saint Joseph? Which saint started the first American religious community of women? Do you know which saint is the patron of nature? Find the answers in the *Saints of North America, Saints and Me!* set and help your child identify with the lives of the saints.

Introduce your children or students to the *Saints and Me!* series as they:

—READ about the lives of the saints and are inspired by their stories.

—PRAY to the saints for their intercession.

—CELEBRATE the saints and relate to their lives.

saints
of north
America

 Kateri Tekakwitha

 Juan Diego

 Rose Philippine
Duchesne

 Damien of Molokai

 Elizabeth Ann Seton

 André Bessette

Belgium

France

Joseph de Veuster was born in Belgium. He lived on a farm with his family. They prayed together every day. Joseph's mom read to them. He liked saint stories the best.

Joseph's big brother joined the Congregation
of the Sacred Hearts of Jesus and Mary.
Joseph wanted to be a priest, too.
"I want to be a missionary priest," he said.

When he was nineteen he joined
the same order as his big brother.
Joseph took the name Damien.
He studied very hard. He prayed that he would
be a good priest—a good missionary priest.

Damien's brother was ordained.
He was sent to the Hawaiian missions,
but he got sick and could not go. Damien asked
to take his place. The Superior General said
yes. The news made Damien very happy.

The ocean trip took many months.
They stopped in the big city of Honolulu.
It was a beautiful place. Damien saw flowers,
palm trees, and colorful birds. He prayed,
"God, help me to do your work here."

Damien finished his studies in Honolulu and
was ordained a priest. People called him
Father Damien. He taught the people about
God. He said Mass and heard confessions.
Father Damien was friendly and cheerful.

Father Damien worked in many villages.
He was strong and a hard worker.
He helped the people build churches and
chapels. He showed them how to farm.
The people loved him very much.

One day Father Damien heard about Molokai.
It was an island. Sick people were sent to
Molokai. The sick people had leprosy,
a serious skin disease. They were called lepers.
Molokai was a lonely place to live.

"Who would like to go to Molokai?"
the bishop asked. "The people there are
very sick." Father Damien said, "I will go.
I will be their priest." He wanted to share
God's love with the lepers.

There was so much to do on Molokai.
Father Damien got to work right away.
He cleaned the church. Now he could say
Mass. He visited the people in their huts.
They prayed together.

Father Damien taught them how to plant crops
and raise animals. "Thank you, Father.
You are kind and good to us," they said.
Father Damien treated the lepers with respect.
They were his family.

"Come to Mass and pray," called Father
Damien. The little church was full of people.
They needed a choir and music, too!
So Father Damien started a choir and a band.

For sixteen years, Father Damien lived and worked with the lepers on Molokai. Father Damien helped build schools and orphanages. He also helped the families build new homes. Volunteers came to help them. Molokai was a better place to live.

Then one day Father Damien found out
he had leprosy, too. "I have more work to do,"
he thought. His faith gave him the strength
to keep working. But he got weaker each day.
Then he had to stay in bed.

Father Damien was happy that other people had come to Molokai to help. He prayed for his friends on Molokai. "Take care of my people," whispered Father Damien. He told those at his bedside, "I will pray for you in heaven."

After Father Damien died, many people heard of his work. More volunteers went to Molokai. People sent money and supplies. Lots of people tried to help. Today, there is a cure for leprosy.

Saint Damien of Molokai,
the "Leper Priest," saw beauty in everyone.
We are all children of God.

*Help the sick
and do your part
to comfort them
with all your heart.*

Dear Jesus,

I love you.

Saint Damien

of Molokai

loved you, too.

He shared your love

with the lepers

on Molokai.

Teach me to love

and respect people.

Amen.

NEW WORDS (Glossary)

Bishop: A priest who is the leader of many churches in a certain area

Leper: A person who has leprosy

Leprosy: A disease that causes nerve damage and sores on the skin

Missionary: A person who teaches the faith or preaches the gospel in a certain place

Order: A religious community of men or women

Orphanage: A home for children who do not have parents

Superior General: The head or leader of a religious order

Village: Small groups of people living near each other; a very small town

Volunteers: People who help without being paid